Temecula Wineries

By Jeff Joseph

Temecula Wineries: The Ultimate Temecula Winery and Temecula Wine Tasting Guidebook: Ultimate Guide to Temecula Wine Country

978-1-60332-071-9

Printed in the United States of America

This book is dedicated to Adriane, Jacob, Lucky, & Bella.

Temecula Valley Wineries A-Z

Alex's Red Barn Winery

39820 Calle Contento
Temecula, CA 92591

951.693.3201
www.redbarnwine.com

Hours

Summer: 11:00 am – 6:00 pm
Winter: 10:00 am – 5:00 pm
Open Saturdays and Sundays and most holidays

Wine List

Red Wines	White Wines	Dessert Wines
Cabernet Sauvignon	Johannisberg	Solera Style
Syrah	Riesling	Sherry
	Muscat Canelli	
	Viognier	
	Sauvignon Blanc	

Wine Tasting

$10.00 – includes seven wines and a free souvenir glass

Wine Club Information

- Receive a shipment of two bottles of wine every month
- 15% discount on wine
- 10% discount in the gift shop
- Free tasting for two whenever you visit the winery

Baily Vineyard & Winery

33440 La Serena Way
Temecula, CA 92591

951-676-9463
www.bailywinery.com

Hours

Monday-Friday: 11:00 am – 5:00 pm
Saturday: 10:00 am – 5:00 pm

Wine List

Red Wines	White/Rosé Wines	Dessert Wines
Sangiovese	Montage	Serenity - Late
Merlot	Chardonnay	Harvest
Cabernet Sauvignon	Semillon	Chardonnay
Cabernet Franc	Riesling	Vintage Port
Meritage	Muscat Blanc	
	Rosé of Cabernet	
	Sauvignon	

Wine Tasting

Regular: $5.00 - Taste 5 different wines, except Cabernet
Sauvignon, Cabernet Franc, Meritage, and Port, and keep
12 oz logo tasting glass.

Premium: $10.00 - Taste any 5 different wines, (no
restrictions) and keep 19 oz logo tasting glass

Wine Club Information

- Receive two bottles of wine, every other month
- Free tasting for two any time you visit the tasting
  room. (Glass not included.)
- 20% off normal winery price on wine purchases no
  matter how many bottles you buy
- 10% off gift items

- 10% off on food and beverages at Carol's Restaurant.
- 10% off on food and beverages at Baily's Fine Dining
- 10% off at Baily's Fine Dining and Front Street Bar & Grill

Restaurants

CAROL'S RESTAURANT

Lunch Hours: Wednesday – Friday - 11:30 am – 2:30 pm
Saturday & Sunday - 11:30 am – 3:00 pm

Carol's has a selection of luncheon salads, sandwiches, grilled fish and steak, and pasta dishes. The wine list features Baily and other Temecula Valley wines, as well as a handful from outside the Valley.

Weddings & Private Events

Baily Vineyard & Winery can accommodate up to 48 guests for private events. Visit their website for more information.

Carol's Restaurant at
Baily Vineyard & Winery

Photo by Adriane Valley

Bella Vista

41220 Calle Contento
Temecula, CA 92591

951-676-5250
www.cilurzowine.com

Hours

Summer: 10:00 am – 6:00 pm
Winter: 10:00 am – 5:00 pm
Open seven days a week.

Wine List

Red Wines	White Wines	Champagne
Petite Syrah Rosé	Muscat Canelli	Bella Vista
Sonata	Riesling	Champagne
Zinfandel	Viognier	
Cabernet Sauvignon	Sauvignon Blanc	
Merlot Reserve	Fumé Blanc	
Petite Syrah	Chardonnay	
Reserve		
Petite Syrah		
White Cabernet		

Wine Tasting

$8.00 – includes five tastes and a free souvenir wine glass

Wine Club Information

- Receive a shipment of two bottles of wine, six times a year
- 20% discount on wine
- Free tasting for two whenever you visit the winery
- Special rates on event tickets

Boorman Vineyards Estate Winery

21630 Ave De Arboles
Murrieta, CA 92562

951-600-9333
www.boormanvineyards.com

Hours

Private tasting and tours available by appointment only

Wine List

<u>Red Wines</u>
Barbera
Cabernet Franc
Cabernet Sauvignon
Merlot
Metaphor

Wine Tasting

Private tasting and tours available by appointment only

Callaway Vineyard & Winery

32720 Rancho California Rd.   800-472-2377
Temecula, CA 92591   www.callawaywinery.com

Hours

10:00 am – 5:00 pm
Open seven days a week.

Wine List

Red Wines	White Wines	Rose Wines
Sangiovese	Chardonnay	Rose of
Cabernet Franc	Pinot Gris	Cabernet
Cabernet Sauvignon	Muscat Canelli	Sauvignon
Old Vine Zinfandel	Sauvignon Blanc	Bela Rose
Dolcetto	Viognier	
A.K.A. (Also Known	Sweet Nancy	
As...Port)		
Meritage		
Merlot		
Syrah		

Wine Tasting & Tours

Complimentary Winery Tours
Weekdays – 11:00 am, 1:00 pm, and 3:00 pm
Weekends - every hour on the hour between 11:00 am and
4:00 pm

Wine Tasting
$10.00 per person – includes six tastes and souvenir wine
glass

Callaway Experience Private Tour & Wine Tasting
$15.00 per person (plus 18% service fee and tax)

Wine Club Information

- Receive two bottles of wine at a 30% discount, every two months
- Complimentary limited wine tasting each time you visit; up to 2 people, excludes logo glass. Guests are accommodated at a discounted fee.
- 25% discount on all wine purchases
- 20% discount on all non-wine merchandise
- 10% discount at Meritage at Callaway
- 10% discount on winery Special Events and Private Group Packages (Monday-Thursday, excludes holidays & weddings)
- Exclusive tasting bar for Legacy Club members on weekends
- One complimentary VIP winery tour and educational wine tasting per year. A two-week minimum advance reservation is required: based on availability. Limited to 4 people total; excludes logo glass
- A bi-monthly newsletter, which includes winemaker notes and winery news & recipes from their Executive Chef with wine pairing suggestions
- Extended member benefits with their affiliate winery, Orfila Vineyard & Winery, located in Escondido. Please call their Wine Club department for arrangements.
- Wine Club Coordinators to assist you with winery visits, reservations and purchases.

Restaurants

MERITAGE AT CALLAWAY

Hours: Lunch – 11:00 am – 4:00 pm
Dinner – 4:00 pm – 8:00 pm

$5.00 Happy Hour Menu - Every Thursday & Friday from 4:00 - 6:00 pm

Executive Chef, Michael Henry, has designed an exciting Tapas menu with a Mediterranean flare. The cuisine will be based on the "small plate" concept of big flavor and variety, with menu selections being paired with the best of what Callaway Winery offers.

Weddings & Private Events

Callaway Vineyard & Winery can accommodate up to 250 guests for private events. Visit their website for more information.

Churon Winery

33233 Rancho California Road   951-694-9071
Temecula, CA 92591   www.churonwinery.com

Hours

10:00 am – 5:00 pm
Open seven days a week

Wine List

Red Wines
Sangiovese Rose
Syrah
Merlot
Cabernet Sauvignon
Cabernet Franc
Petite Verdot Malbec

White Wines
Chardonnay
Viognier

Wine Tasting

$10.00 per person – includes six tastes and a souvenir logo glass

Wine Club Information

- 2 Bottles of Churon's exclusive wine shipped to your door every 2 months
- 15% off all rooms in the Inn and upgrades during the weekdays (Membership active 4 days after initial sign up)
- 15% off gift boutique merchandise
- 15% off wine purchased in Winery and 20% off case orders
- Complimentary wine tasting for you and a guest
- Discounts on special event packages
- Access to special release wines

- Invitations to special artist and winery events

Accommodations

INN AT CHURON WINERY

Rates: $149.95 – $350.00/per night

French Style Chateau Bed and Breakfast with sixteen spacious vineyard view rooms and six enormous suites. Rooms and suites offer gas burning fireplaces, Jacuzzi bathtub for two, elegant French furnishings and a private balcony or terrace overlooking beautiful gardens, fountains and vineyards.

Weddings & Private Events

Churon Winery can accommodate up to 250 guests for private events. Call for more information.

Cougar Vineyard & Winery

39870 De Portola Road
Temecula, CA 92592

951-491-0825
www.cougarvineyards.com

Hours

11:00 am – 6:00 pm
Open seven days a week

Wine List

Red Wines	White Wines	Sparkling Wines
Sangiovese	Chardonnay	Sparkling Cougar
Montepulciano	Muscat Canelli	
Malbec	Riesling	
Cabernet Sauvignon	Pink Cougar	
Primitivo	Cortese	
Anglianico		
Meritage		
Merlot		
Cabernet Franc		

Wine Tasting

$10.00 per person - includes 7-8 tastes and souvenir glass

Tours

Tours are available during normal business hours. Call for more details.

Wine Club Information

- Two specially selected bottles of wine each quarter from winemakers Rick and Jennifer Buffington. Shipments are processed in March, June, September and December. Shipments occasionally include wine not available to the general public.
- Special Events held for Wine Club Members only.
- 20% discount on all wines purchased from their web site.
- Access to new releases and sales
- Home or office delivery
- Winemaker notes, recipes and quarterly updates
- It's free to join and you can cancel at any time after receiving the second shipment. All cancellations must be verified 15 days prior to the next shipments date.

Weddings & Private Events

Cougar Vineyard & Winery can accommodate up to 75 guests for private events. Call for more information.

Doffo Wines

36083 Summitville
Temecula, CA 92592

714-715-6610
www.doffowines.com

Hours

10:00 am – 5:00 pm
Open Friday through Sunday and Holidays

Wine List

Red Wines	White Wines	Library Wines
Mistura	Sauvignon Blanc	Port
Shiraz	Viognier	Magnum
Cabernet Sauvignon		Los Nietos
Malbec		

Wine Tasting

Standard - $15.00 per person – includes six wines
VIP - $25.00 per person – includes five premium wines
and choice of three whites
Verticals: (Different vintages of the same varietal) $45.00-
Each, Minimum group of 10 people. It will be conducted by
Winemaker, Marcelo Doffo in the Private Tasting Room.

Wine Club Information

- Receive their hand crafted wine delivered to your door at a 10% discount.
- Complimentary tasting for yourself and 1 guest anytime you visit Doffo Winery
- Special invitations to "Members Only" Events
- Email updates on new releases, special events and winemaker specials
- No Membership Fee is required

Tasting Room at Falkner Winery   Photo by Jeff Joseph

Falkner Winery

40620 Calle Contento
Temecula, CA 92591

951-676-8231
www.falknerwinery.com

Hours

10:00 am – 5:00 pm
Open seven days a week

Wine List

Red Wines
Amante
Syrah
Meritage
Port
Merlot
Cabernet Sauvignon
Luscious Lips

White Wines
Sweet Loretta
Sauvignon Blanc
Viognier
Riesling
Chardonnay

Wine Tasting

Regular Tasting: 5 wines from regular list for $8.00 per person ($10.00 with souvenir glass)

Premium Tasting: 3 premium wines for $10.00 per person ($12.00 with souvenir glass)

Combo Tasting: 5 wines from regular list + 3 premium wines w/souvenir glass for $16.00 per person

Port Tasting $2.00

Single Regular Taste $2.00

Premium Taste $3.00

Tours

Public Tours of the winery are conducted at 11:00 am and 2:00 pm every weekend and cost only $5.00 per person.

Wine Club Information

- Taste in the exclusive VIP Room on weekends
- FREE weekend tours at designated times
- FREE shipping for wine purchases above $150.00
- FREE Wine Tasting Classes
- Free combo tasting plus port for member, spouse and 2 guests
- Bimonthly shipments of 3 bottles of wine for less than $50.00 plus tax (if applicable) and shipping
- 30% discount from retail on all wine purchases at the winery and on our web site.
- FREE shipping for wine purchases above $150.00
- FREE Wine Tasting Classes
- Receive new and limited release wines before the public
- Invitation to special Wine Club Only events
- Receive other special offers and discounts. Shipments based on retail price minus a 10% Wine Club discount

Restaurants

THE PINNACLE RESTAURANT AT FAULKNER WINERY

Hours: Monday-Thursday from 11:30 am-4:00 pm and Friday-Sunday 11:30 am-2:30 pm

The Pinnacle will offer great panoramic views, outstanding Mediterranean style food, and high quality service for lunches 7 days a week. Set on a 1,500 foot hilltop, The Pinnacle will offer customers seating either in the air conditioned indoors or on the open-air outdoor balcony.

The restaurant will also serve as an evening wedding and banquet venue.

Weddings & Private Events

Falkner Winery can accommodate up to 175+ people for private events. Visit website or call for more information

.

Filsinger Vineyards & Winery

39050 De Portola Road   951-302-6363
Temecula, CA 92592   www.filsingerwinery.com

Hours

Friday - 11:00 am - 4:00 pm
Weekends - 10:00 am - 5:00 pm

Wine List

Red Wines	White/Rose Wines	Sparkling Wines
Cabernet Sauvignon	Charvinier	Diamond
Tempranillo	Chardonnay	Cuvee
Merlot	Fume Blanc	Strawberry
Syrah	Gewürztraminer	Rose
Zinfandel "Old Vine"	Orange Muscat	
Sweet Desire	Riesling	
	Viognier	
	White Cabernet	

Wine Tasting

$4.00 per person – includes five tastes

Tours

Tours by appointment only

Foote Print Winery

36650 Glen Oaks Road
Temecula, CA 92592

951-265-9951
www.footeprintwinery.com

Hours

Fridays – 12:00 pm to 5:00 pm
Weekends – 10:00 am to 5:00 pm

Wine List

<u>Red Wines</u>
Merlot
Syrah
Cabernet Sauvignon
Red Foote
Zinfandel
Zinfandel Port

Wine Tasting

$10.00 per person – includes six tastes and a souvenir logo glass

Tours

Winery Tours by appointment only

Wine Club Information

- 20% discount on wine
- Two shipments of six bottles each per year
- Wine club members taste for free when they visit
- Wine club member guests taste for $6.00

Frangipani Estate Winery

39750 De Portola Road   951-699-8845
Temecula, CA 92592   www.frangipaniwinery.com

Hours

Monday-Sunday 10:00 am-5:00 pm

Wine List

<u>Red Wines</u>
Sangiovese
Grenache
Zinfandel
Cabernet Franc
Merlot
Claret
Cabernet Sauvignon
Petite Syrah
Zinfandel

<u>White/Rose Wines</u>
Viognier
Sauvignon Blanc
Grenache Rose
Riesling

Wine Tasting

$10.00 per person - includes 7 tastes

Tours

Tours by appointment only

Wine Club Information

- Four bottles of wine, hand selected by their Winemaker, delivered to your doorstep 3 times a year.
- Complimentary tasting for yourself and two guests any time you visit Frangipani Winery.

- 20% discount bottles of wine and 25% discount by the case.
- Special event discount .... Winemaker's dinner, Private Barrel Tasting and other "Wine Club Members Only" events.
- Frangipani Newsletter, featuring special recipes for wine pairing, upcoming winery and community events, new release information and winemaker notes will be included with your shipment.

Gershon Bachus Vintners (GBV)

37750 De Portola Road   877-458-8428
Temecula, CA 92592   www.gershonbachus.com

Hours

Friday-Sunday 11:00 am-6:00 pm

Wine List

Red Wines
Cabernet Sauvignon
Villa Vino Rosso
Zinfandel

White Wines
Villa Vino White Duet–
Chardonnay/Sauvignon Blanc
Four Four Two

Wine Tasting

$25.00 per person – includes five tastes
By Appointment only
Weekday tastings are a minimum of eight people.
Superior white and red varietals - $30.00 per person

Wine Club Information

Coming Soon!
Call winery for details.

Weddings & Private Events

Gershon Bachus Vintners can accommodate up to 250
guests for private events. Call for more information.

Hart Winery

41300 Avenida Biona   951-676-6300
Temecula, CA 92593   www.thehartfamilywinery.com

Hours

9:00 am - 4:30 pm
Open seven days a week

Wine List

Red Wines	White Wines	Dessert Wines
Syrah Rose	Viognier	Aleatico
Barbera		
Tempranillo		
Zinfandel Huis		
Syrah		
Merlot		
Stonelake Merlot		
Cabernet Sauvignon		
Cabernet Franc		
VR Syrah		
VR Cabernet		
Sauvignon		
Zinfandel Old Vine		

Wine Tasting

$5.00 - 6 wines and free souvenir logo glass
$10.00 - includes the Reserve and Limited wine selection

Wine Club Information

- Receive a shipment of two wines, four times a year
- Free tasting for you and up to three guests every time you visit the winery

- 20% Discount on bottles, and 20% off tasting room merchandise
- Be a guest at Wine Club members-only events

Keyways Vineyard & Winery

37338 De Portola Road
Temecula, CA 92592

951-302-7888
www.keywayswine.com

Hours

10:00 am – 5:00 pm
Summer Hours 10:00 am – 6:00 pm
Open seven days a week

Wine List

Red Wines	White Wines	Dessert Wines
Cabernet Sauvignon	Sauvignon Blanc	First Crush
Syrah	Riesling	Sweet Surrender
Frolich		Port
Barbera		Ice Wine
Spellbound		
Merlot		
Zinfandel		
Tempranillo		

Wine Tasting

$10.00 per person – includes six tastes
Premium Tasting $15.00 per person – includes six tastes
(three premium) and a souvenir wine glass and dessert
glass

Tours

Tours are available on weekends at 10:30am and 11:30am.

Wine Club Information

Club Rewards receive 2 select Keyways wines in 6-8 shipments per year plus, suggested food pairing with recipes and our wine maker's notes.

- 20% discount on wine and non-wine items.
- Our standard shipment is 2 select wines. Alternatively, you may opt for 4, 6 or 12 bottles per shipment of the selected wines. With the 6 bottle option, you will receive a 25% discount on both wine and non-wine items and a 30% discount if you select the 12 bottle option.
- Complimentary wine tasting for member and one guest with each visit to Keyways.
- Special invitations for exclusive member-only events.
- 10% event discount on ticketed Keyways events.

Weddings & Private Events

Keyways Vineyard & Winery can accommodate up to guests for private events. Call for more information.

La Cereza Vineyard & Winery

34567 Rancho California Road
Temecula, CA 92591

951-699-6961
www.lacerezawinery.com

Hours

10:00 am – 5:00 pm
Open seven days a week

Wine List

Red Wines	White & Rose Wines	Dessert Wines
Sangiovese	Chardonnay	Gewurztraminer
Rojo Novato	Pinot Grigio La Cereza	Summer's End
Hope La Cereza	Viognier	
Garnacha La Cereza	Girlfriends	Champagne
Zinfandel	Miracles	VR La Cereza
Merlot	Happen La Cereza	VR La Cereza
Cabernet Sauvignon	White Zinfandel	Raspberry
Shiraz	Rose of Garnacha	Sparkling Peach Girls
Tempranillo La Cereza		
Vaquero del Vino		

Wine Tasting

$10.00 per person for six tastes and a logo glass
Passport Ticket - $15.00 per person which entitles you to
six tastings and a logo glass at La Cereza and at the sister
winery, Maurice Car'rie

Tours

La Cereza offers tours and tastings for groups of 15 or more with advance reservation. The charge for a tour and tasting, which includes a souvenir logo glass and tax, is $18.00 per guest

Wine Club Information

- All Red, All White, Mixed: 3 pack, 6 pack or 12 pack
- Complimentary tasting for you and 3 guests at La Cereza and Maurice Car'rie wineries
- 20% discount on wines
- 30% discount on cases
- 10% discount on boutique items
- VIP tasting area with exclusive member glasses

Weddings & Private Events

La Cereza can accommodate up to 800 guests for private events. Visit website for more information.

Leonesse Cellars

38311 De Portola Road
Temecula, CA 92592

951-302-7601
www.leonessecellars.com

Hours

10:00 am-5:00 pm
Open seven days a week

Wine List

Red Wines
Syrah
Merlot
Melange De Rêves
Meritage
Cabernet Sauvignon
Cabernet Franc-Merlot
Zinfandel
SS Meritage
Cinsaut Port

White & Rosé Wines
Pinot Grigio
Sauvignon Blanc
Chardonnay
VSS Chardonnay
Riesling
Muscat Canelli
White Merlot
Rosé of Cabernet
Sauvignon

Wine Tasting

$10.00 per person for six tastes and a logo glass
Passport Ticket - $15.00 per person which entitles you to
six tastings and a logo glass at La Cereza and at the sister
winery, Maurice Car'rie

Wine Club Information

- Three bottles of Leonesse wine every three months
  chosen especially for you by our winemaker,
  including limited and pre-release wines, library
  wines, and "Club Member Only" wines. The price

per shipment is $50.00 (plus shipping and sales tax), which will automatically be billed to your credit card

- Winemaker's Tasting Notes and food pairing tips for each wine included in the current shipment, as well as great recipes to prepare and serve with your favorite Leonesse wines
- 25% discount on all reorders of the current wine club shipment wines, as well as other special offers included with each shipment available to club members only
- 25% discount on all wine purchases made at the winery, through our online store, or via telephone
- 10% discount per person on all special events hosted by Leonesse Cellars
- 10% for Merchandise and at Block 5
- Complimentary wine tasting for yourself and up to three guests every time you visit the winery
- Special invitations to "Member Only" events at the winery

Restaurants

BLOCK 5 RESTAURANT

Hours:
Lunch: Wednesday-Sunday from 11:30 am to 3:30 pm
Dinner: Friday 5:30 pm to 9:30 pm

The menu will feature such items as Rib Eye Medallions, Grilled Lamb, Monterey Caesar Salad, Honey Curry Chicken with Flat bread, and much more.

Weddings & Private Events

Leonesse Cellars can accommodate up to 200 guests for private events. Call for more information.

Longshadow Ranch Vineyard & Winery

39847 Calle Contento   951-587-6221
Temecula, CA 92591   www.longshadowranchwinery.com

Hours

Monday - Friday 12:00 pm – 5:00 pm
Saturday 10:00 am – 5:00 pm
Sunday 10:00 am – 5:00 pm

Wine List

Red Wines
Cabernet Franc
Outlaw Red - Gunslinger's
 Reserve
Cabernet Sauvignon - New
 Release
Cinsault
Syrah
White Merlot
Merlot – Unfiltered
Reata Red

White Wines
White Feather
 Chardonnay
Muscat

Dessert Wines
Ponderosa Port

Wine Tasting

$10.00 per person – includes five tastes and a souvenir
logo glass

Wine Club Information

- Two bottles of our wine shipped to you every other
  month
- Enjoy our family oriented ambiance, special events,
  live music on weekends

- FREE premium wine tasting
- 15% discount on wine purchases.
- Reduced pricing on facility fees for weddings and other private parties and special events

Weddings & Private Events

Longshadow Ranch Vineyard & Winery can accommodate up to 250 guests for private events. Call for more information or send an email to info@longshadowranchwinery.com.

Maurice Car'rie Vineyard & Winery

34225 Rancho California Rd
Temecula, CA 92592

951-676-1711
www.mauricecarriewinery.com

Hours

10:00 am to 5:00 pm
Open seven days a week

Wine List

Red Wines
Cabernet Sauvignon
Merlot
Cody's Crush
Sangiovese

White & Rose Wines
Muscat Canelli
Sauvignon Blanc
Chardonnay
Chenin Blanc
Riesling
Heather's Mist
Sweet Christa's
Sara Bella
White Zinfandel

Dessert Wines
Cream Sherry

Champagne
Pineapple
 Champagne

Wine Tasting

$10.00 per person - includes six tastings and a logo glass.
Passport Tasting, $15.00 per person includes six tastings
and a logo glass at Maurice Car'rie and at the sister winery,
La Cereza

Wine Club Information

- Complimentary tasting for you and 3 guests at
  Maurice Car'rie and La Cereza
- 3 pack, 6 pack or 12 pack

41

- 20% discount on wines
- 30% discount on cases
- 10% discount on boutique items
- VIP tasting area with exclusive member glasses
- One of the only wine clubs to offer a unique way to experience our exceptional wines

Tours

$18.00 per guest includes tour, tasting, and souvenir logo glass

Weddings & Private Events

Maurice Car'rie Vineyard & Winery can accommodate up to 300 guests for private events.

Visit website for more information or send an email to specialevents@mauricecarriewinery.com

Miramonte Winery

33410 Rancho California Rd
Temecula, CA 92591

951-506-5500
www.miramontewinery.com

Hours

Monday – Thursday 11:00 am – 6:00 pm
Friday & Saturday 11:00 am - Late

Wine List

Red Wines	White Wines	Sparkling Wines
Sangiovese	Semillon	Miramonte Winery Grand Reserve Brut
Three Block Shiraz	Sauvignon Blanc	
Merlot	White Rhapsody	
Four Torch	Viognier	
Cabernet Sauvignon	Chardonnay	Miramonte Grand Reserve Blanc de Noirs
Opulente	Grenache Rose	
Old Vine Zinfandel	Riesling	
Syrah		
Numero Uno		
Sangria		

Wine Tasting

$10.00 per person – includes six tastes and a logo glass.

Passport Tasting $15.00 per person – includes six tastings and a logo glass at Maurice Car'rie and at the sister winery, La Cereza

Wine Club Information

- Receive two carefully selected, handcrafted wines, along with our beautiful newsletter which keeps you informed about our artfully crafted wines, any new

43

developments in the vineyard, and the latest happenings here at the winery

- 20% - 25% discount on wine
- VIP access and treatment at the winery
- 10% -15% off all merchandise and event tickets

Mount Palomar Winery

33820 Rancho California Rd   951-676-5047
Temecula, CA 92591   www.mountpalomar.com

Hours

Summer Hours:
Monday – Thursday 10:00 am - 6:00 pm
Friday - Sunday 10:00 am - 7:00 pm

Wine List

Red Wines	White Wines	Dessert Wines
Cinsaut	Viognier	Riesling
Sangiovese	Sauvignon Blanc	Solanus
Shorty's Bistro Red	Chardonnay	Port
Cabernet Sauvignon	Chardonnay	Solera Cream
Cabernet Franc	Cortese	Sherry
Merlot	Sangiovese Rosé	
Cloudbreak	Shorty's Bistro	
Syrah	White	
Trovato		
Übervin		
Meritage		
Petit Verdot		

Wine Tasting

$10.00 – includes six tastes

Tours

Tours are available by appointment only at this time.
Please call 800-854-5177 ext. 119 to schedule a tour

Wine Club Information

- An informative newsletter with current winery news, special events and gourmet recipes.
- Eight (8) complimentary tasting coupons with every shipment for you and your guests to use when visiting the tasting room.
- Invitations to special events including our Wine Club Barbeque, Wine Club pick-up parties and Barrel Tasting for members only.
- Access to our "Members Only" tasting bar on Saturday and Sunday.
- Two exclusive Mount Palomar logo glasses and a logo waiter's wine opener.
- An annual, complimentary, Estate Club Members Only, wine reception.
- Twenty-five percent discount on wine and Gift Center merchandise purchases.
  Note: Discounts do not apply to Best of Vintage and Cloudbreak wines and consignment or custom art work.
- Ten percent discount on food purchases in our deli.

Weddings & Private Events

Mount Palomar Winery can accommodate up to 150 guests for private events.

Visit their website or call for detailed information.

Oak Mountain Winery

36522 Via Verde
Temecula, CA 92592

951-699-9102
www.oakmountainwinery.com

Hours

11:00 am-5:00 pm
Open seven days a week

Wine List

Red Wines	White Wines	Blush Wines
Merlot	Chardonnay	Rosé of
Miscela di	"No Oak	Cabernet
Sangiovese	Chardonnay"	Sauvignon
Cabernet Sauvignon	Sauvignon Blanc	White Merlot
Meritage		
Zinfandel	Sparkling Wines	
Port	Brut Champagne	

Wine Tasting

Regular: $10.00 per person – includes six tastes and a
souvenir logo glass

VIP Tasting: Very exclusive candlelit, private tasting
surrounded by oak wine barrels in our barrel room. The
tasting will be conducted by our winemaker / owner upon
availability and will include six wines and appetizer
pairings. The price including the Reidel crystal stem is
$20.00 per person or $15.00 per person if you elect not to
keep the Reidel crystal stem. The tasting is by reservation
with a maximum of 12 people. Reservations can be made
on line or by calling the winery at 951-699-9102

Wine Club Information

- 2 bottles of Oak Mountain wine selected by Steve Andrews our winemaker shipped directly to you four times throughout the year.
- The opportunity to attend winery events yearly, hosted by our wine maker Steve Andrews.
- Membership discounts of up to 20% on all wine. (Gold Club 25%)
- Free sampling in the Tasting Room

Palumbo Family Vineyards & Winery

40150 Barksdale Cir.
Temecula, CA 92591

951-676-7900
www.palumbofamilyvineyards.com

Hours

Friday 12:00 pm-5:00 pm
Saturday 10:00 am-5:00 pm
Sunday 10:00 am-5:00 pm
Weekdays by appointment

Wine List

Red Wines
Merlot
Cabernet Sauvignon
Shiraz
Tre Fratelli
Sangiovese
Cabernet Franc

White & Rose Wines
Viognier
Rose

Wine Tasting

$7.00 per person – includes five tastes
$10.00 per person – includes five tastes and a souvenir
logo glass

Wine Club Information

Not accepting new members. Waiting list only.

Tasting Room at Ponte Family Estate
Winery

Photo by Jeff Joseph

Tasting Room at Ponte Family Estate
Winery

Photo by Jeff Joseph

Ponte Family Estate Winery

35053 Rancho California Rd
Temecula, CA 92591

951-694-8855
www.pontewinery.com

Hours

10:00 am - 5:00 pm
Open seven days a week

Wine List

Red Wines
Dolcetto
Super Tuscan
Cabernet Sauvignon
Merlot
Beverino
Nebbiolo
Ponte Barbera
Holiday Reserve Zinfandel
 Magnum

White Wines
Graciela
Ariana
Pinot Grigio
Chardonnay
Riesling
Moscato
Fume Blanc
Rose Spumante
Fiorella
Juliet
Isabel

Wine Tasting

Monday – Thursday $10.00 per person
Friday - Sunday $12.00 per person

Tasting includes 6 wine tastes and a souvenir Ponte logo
glass

Tours

Tour & Tasting - $15.00 per person

Tours are given every Saturday and Sunday at 1:00 pm and 3:00 pm. Arrive 10 minutes before the tour and purchase your tickets at the cashier desk. For private tours, reservations are required and a minimum of 4 guests per tour is requested.

The Barrel Room Experience
$75.00 - $85.00 per person, depending on menu selection

Wine Club Information

- 20% discount on 2-3 bottles of specially selected Ponte Family Estate wines, shipped directly to you eight times a year. Two of the shipments are special packages that include two bottles of our newly released specialty wine. The selections are sent to you along with our informative newsletter, which includes wine notes and savory food recipes to complement the wines created by our Executive Chef.
- 20% discount on all wines purchased at the winery or from our Online Store.
- 20% discount on all items sold in our Marketplace or from our Online Store.
- 10% discount at our popular Smokehouse Restaurant for your entire party.
- 10% discount on private events booked at Ponte Family Estate, Monday through Thursday. Treat your guests to private luncheons, dinners, and receptions in our beautiful Tent Pavilion, Barrel Room, or Wine Club VIP Room (holiday periods and weddings excluded).
- 10% discount at Ponte Winery ticketed special events.

- Free wine tasting for you and one guest each time you visit the winery. You and your guest will enjoy access to the members-only VIP Tasting Room and taste wine in our finest glassware.
- Invitations to Wine Club Members-Only events, such as our new release parties and holiday shopping nights.
- Priority reservations at our Winemaker Dinners, concerts, and holiday parties, including our annual Grape Stomping Festival and New Year's Eve Extravaganza.
- Our Members-Only Temecula Wine Country concierge service, which provides recommendations for local restaurants, hotels, hot air balloon rides, and group tours. Simply call or email us for "insider information" on what's going on in Wine Country.

Restaurant

THE SMOKEHOUSE RESTAURANT

Hours:
Brunch Hours: Sunday 10:00 am – 2:00 pm
Lunch Hours: Monday – Saturday 11:00 am – 5:00 pm
Dinner Hours: Friday – Saturday 6:00 pm – 9:00 pm
Sunday 3:00 pm – 7:00 pm

The Smokehouse Restaurant menu changes with the season and reflects the influences of area vineyards, local farmers' markets, and their own Estate wines.

Weddings & Private Events

Ponte Family Estate Winery can accommodate up to 500 guests for private events. Visit website for more information.

Rancho de Andallusia Vineyard & Winery

32828 Wolf Store Road
Temecula, CA 92592

951-302-1800
www.andallusia.com

Hours

Wednesday - Thursday 3:00-8:00 pm
Friday 3:00 – 9:00 pm
Saturday 2:00 – 9:00 pm
Sunday 1:00 – 5:00 pm

Wine List

Red Wines
Syrah
Cabernet Sauvignon
Sangiovese
Zinfandel
Merlot

White & Rosé Wines
Malbec
Riesling
Chardonnay
Fume Blanc
White Merlot

Wine Club Information:

- Complimentary wine tasting for yourself and a guest every time you visit the winery.
- A 20% discount is available to members on all wines purchased at our winery.
- A 25% discount is given to members on all purchases of full case quantities of any wine.

Robert Renzoni Vineyards

37350 De Portola Road
Temecula, CA 92592

951-302-8466
www.robertrenzonivineyards.com

Hours

11:00 am – 6:00 pm
Open seven days a week

Wine List

<u>Red Wines</u>
Concerto
Sangiovese
Cabernet Sauvignon
Old Vine Zinfandel

<u>White & Rosé Wines</u>
Pinot Grigio
Chardonnay
Bellisimo
Moscato
La Rosa

Wine Tasting

$11.00 per person

Tours

Tours & Private tastings are available by advance appointment only.

Wine Club Information

- 25% off normal winery prices in our tasting room, telephone orders, and online store
- 25% off all gift items
- Discounts on Winemaker dinners & functions
- Discounts on new releases, special bottlings, & library wines

- Private invitations to "Member Only" events at the winery
- Food pairing suggestions for each wine included in the current shipment
- Pre-release notification. You can get our new releases before anyone else!
- Complimentary wine tasting for yourself and one guest every time you visit the winery

Weddings & Private Events

The Robert Renzoni Vineyards Tuscan Villa is scheduled for completion in 2009. Call for more information about hosting a private event once the facility is completed.

South Coast Winery Resort & Spa

34843 Rancho California Rd   951-587-9463
Temecula, CA 92591   www.wineresort.com

Hours

10:00 am to 6:00 pm
Open seven days a week

Wine List

Red Wines
Zinfandel
Merlot
Syrah
Cabernet Sauvignon
Meritage
Old Vine Zinfandel
Sangiovese
Grenache
Big Red Table Wine
Romanza

Sparkling Wines
Brut Sparkling Wine
Extra Dry Sparkling Wine
Sparkling Syrah (Ruby Cuvee)

White & Rosé Wines
GVR
Sauvignon Blanc
Chardonnay
Riesling
Viognier
Chardonnay Sans Chene
Gewürztraminer
Muscat Canelli
Roussane
Sweet Maggie
Grenache Rose
Merlot Rose
Cabernet Rose

Dessert Wines
Black Jack Port

Wine Tasting

Five tastes for $10.00 per person ($5.00 per person for
South Coast Wine Club members) with souvenir glass
included or try our specially selected Reserve selection with
five tastes for $15.00 per person ($7.50 per person for
South Coast Wine Club members). Tasting Ticket sales
stop at 5:45 pm

Tasting Room at South Coast Winery　　　　　　Photo by Jeff Joseph

Vineyard Rose Patio at South Coast　　　　　　Photo by Jeff Joseph
Winery

Tours

$20.00 per person - Tours are held daily at 10:30 a.m. each day, and an extra tour is held on Saturdays and Sundays at 12:30 p.m. For more details or to arrange a private tour for a group of 15 or more, send an email to WineClub@WineResort.com or call 866.994.6379

Wine Club Information

- 25% Discount 12 Bottles or More
- 20% Discount on 1-11 Bottles of Wine
- 20% Discount at the GrapeSeed Spa all day every Wednesday
  and 10% Mondays thru Thursdays
- 15% Discount on Gift Shop Merchandise
- 10% Discount on Overnight Villa Stays
- 10% Discount at Vineyard Rose Restaurant for up to 4 people
- 10% Discount at South Coast Winery Restaurant in Orange County
  for up to 4 people

Restaurant

VINEYARD ROSE

Hours:
Breakfast: 7:00 am to 10:45 am daily
Lunch: 11:30 am to 3:00 pm Monday - Friday
　　　　11:30 am to 3:30 pm Saturday and Sunday

Limited Lunch Menu:
　　　　3:00 pm to 5:00 pm Monday - Friday
　　　　3:30 pm to 5:00 pm Saturday and Sunday

Dinner: 5:30 pm to 9:00 pm Sunday - Thursday
　　　　5:30 pm to 10:00 pm Friday and Saturday

Chef Alessandro Serni, from Tuscany himself, has created breakfast, lunch and dinner menus that have received rave reviews. An extensive wine list, showcasing vintages from South Coast, the region and the globe, compliments Chef Serni's dishes. Restaurant hours are seasonal; dinner reservations recommended; semi-private dining room and private chef's table available for groups and are designed to impress.

Accommodations

76 spacious, richly appointed villas with no common walls. Unwind in 575 to 1,150 square feet, with a fireplace, soothing spa tub, peaceful terrace tucked away in the vineyards...

Rates: Starting at $299.00/nt

Call or visit website for special packages

Spa

GrapeSeed Spa Services include: massage, skin care, salon, fitness, body rituals

Packages start at $235.00
Yoga & Pilates classes available from $12.00

Weddings & Private Events

South Coast Winery Resort & Spa can accommodate up to 500 guests for private events.

Visit website for most updated information.

Stuart Cellars

33515 Rancho California Rd
Temecula, CA 92591

951-676-6414
www.stuartcellars.com

Hours

10:00 am - 5:00 pm
Open seven days a week

Wine List

Red Wines	White Wines	Dessert
Cabernet Franc	Callista	Muscat
Cabernet Sauvignon	Chardonnay	White Port
Long Valley Red	Riesling	Port
Malbec	Sauvignon Blanc	
Merlot	Viognier	
Pinot Noir	White Merlot	
Sangiovese		
Tatria		
Tempranillo		
Zinfandel		

Wine Tasting

$10.00 per person – includes five tastes and a souvenir
logo glass

Tours

Tours are available on weekends by appointment only. The
tour and tasting is $15.00 per person.

Wine Club Information

- Complimentary tasting at the Winery for yourself and up to 2 guests.
- Advance notice and invitations to Winery events.
- Special Member Only wines
- 10% Discounts on Events (excluding weddings).
- No Membership Fee. You can cancel at any time in writing after receiving <u>two</u> shipments.
- Discounts are as follows:
    - 30% discount on Our Ultra-premium wine shipped directly to your door every other month.
    - 40% discount on all reorders of the current wine shipment in that selection month.
    - 30 % discount on all wine purchases of twelve (12) bottles or more.
    - 20% discount on all wine purchases of eleven (11) bottles or less.
    - 10% discount on all other gift shop merchandise.

Weddings & Private Events

Stuart Cellars can accommodate up to 350 people for private events.

Visit their website for more information.

Temecula Hills Winery

47200 De Portola Road
Temecula, CA 92592

951-767-3450
www.temeculahillswinery.com

Hours

11:00 am to 5:00 pm

Wine List

Red Wines
Cabernet Sauvignon
Barbera
Zinfandel
Tempranillo
Tenacious
Syrah
Mourvedre
Grenache
Ed's Red
Dominique
Raspberry Champagne
Tempranillo/Grenache Port

White & Rosé Wines
Viognier
Chardonnay
Muscat Canelli
Vigeant

Wine Tasting

$10.00 per person – includes six tastes and a souvenir logo glass

Tours

Tours by appointment only

Wine Club Information

- 2, 4, 6 or 12 bottles of Temecula Hills Winery wine selected by Steve Andrews our winemaker shipped directly to you four times throughout the year
- The opportunity to attend winery events yearly, hosted by our wine maker Steve Andrews
- Membership discounts of 20% on all wine
- 12 bottle wine club members receive 30% off their wine club purchases
- Free sampling in our Tasting Room

Thornton Winery

32575 Rancho California Rd   951-699-0099
Temecula, CA 92591   www.thorntonwine.com

Hours

10:00 am - 5:00 pm
Open seven days a week

Wine List

Red Wines
Zinfandel
Sangiovese
Rose
Cabernet Sauvignon
Merlot
Syrah
Cabernet-Merlot

Champagnes
Brut Reserve
Brut Reserve Natural
Brut
Blanc de Noir
Cuvee de Frontignan
Almondage
Cuvee Rouge

White Wines
Chardonnay – Sans
 Oak
Gewurztraminer
Riesling
White Zinfandel
Sauvignon Blanc
Chardonnay
Moscato
Viognier

Wine Tasting

$10.00-$17.00 per person - include four tastes

Tours

Tours are available free of charge weekends only
11:00 am, 12:30 pm, 2:00 pm, 4:00 pm

Private tour and tasting

Available for groups of 15 or more. $15.00 per person
Private tour and tasting includes:
• Private tour of the winery
• 3 wines
• 1 champagne
• Bread and goat cheese/cream cheese spread

Wine Club Information

Reserve Club:
- Full or Mixed Case of Varietal Wines and/or Champagnes. Select 12 bottles of your choice from the wines and champagnes listed.
- Two Coupons toward Champagne Jazz Tickets $104.00 value. (may not be combined with any other offer)
- Two Coupons toward Cafe Champagne Meals $84.00 value. (holidays excluded)
- 15% off Champagne Jazz Tickets Up to 4 people per concert, unlimited visits.
- 15% off at Cafe Champagne Up to 4 people per visit, unlimited visits. (private parties and holidays excluded)
- 15% off at the Gift Shop Off all regularly priced items. (sale items excluded)
- 15% off Special Events
- 10% off Banquets (weddings excluded)
- VIP Member Pricing: 20% off Bottle Purchases, 25% off Case Purchases (gift shop purchases only)
- Two free tastings each visit, 15% off additional tastings

- Free tours on weekends.
- Exclusive Parties with John and Steve Thornton

Club de Vin:
- Two bottles of carefully selected, hand-crafted wines every other month.
- 10% off Champagne Jazz Tickets
- 10% off Café Champagne.
- 10% off at Gift Shop Off all regularly priced items.
- 10% off Special Events.
- 10% off Banquets (weddings excluded).
- 20% off Bottle Purchases - VIP Member Pricing; 25% off Case Purchases (Gift Shop purchases only).
- Two Free Tastings Each Visit, 10% off Additional Tastings.
- Free tours on weekends.
- Exclusive Parties with John & Steve Thornton Complimentary for Club Members.
- Special Discounts on Pre-Released Wine $30.00 - $60.00 per shipment, plus tax & shipping.
- Newsletter with notes from the Owners, Winemaker and Executive Chef.
- Personal Assistant/Contact to assist with any needs.

Wedding & Private Events

Thornton Winery can accommodate up to 350 guests for private events. Visit website or call for more information.

Restaurant

CAFÉ CHAMPAGNE

Hours:
Lunch: 11:00 am – 3:30 pm
Dinner: 5:00 pm – 9:00 pm

Café Champagne with their dedicated staff's expertise and artfully designed menu, has won the Gold Award for Contemporary Cuisine for eleven consecutive years from the Southern California Restaurant Writers Association. "Four Stars for Cuisine" and "Four Stars for the Wine List" were awarded by the California Restaurant Writers Association.

Wiens Family Cellars

35055 Via Del Ponte
Temecula, CA 92592

951-694-9892
www.wienscellars.com

Hours

10:00 am-5:00 pm
Open seven days a week

Wine List

Red Wines
Sangiovese
Pinot Noir
Cabernet Franc
Syrah
Tempranillo-Petite Syrah
Reflection
Ruby Port
Crowded
Cabernet Sauvignon

White Wines
Malvasia Bianca
Chardonnay
Viognier
Dulce Maria
White Port
Pinot Gris

Sparkling Wines
Sparkling Amour De
 L'Orange
Sparkling Cosmopolitan

Wine Tasting

6 Tastes and the Glass for $10.00 per person
Wine Club Room and Outdoor Tasting Bar Open
Weekends 10:00 am – 4:00 pm

Tours

Free Tours - Saturdays and Sundays at 11:30 am

Wine Club Information

- Receive two pre-released, premium, red wines before they are available to the public, 6 times a year.
- Receive a 20% discount on all wines and merchandise from our tasting room and 25% off all case purchases.
- Complimentary wine tasting for you and a guest for the lifetime of your membership and get your tasting fee refunded when you sign up
- VIP Status - Invitations to wine club exclusive events and discounts on winery sponsored events

Wedding & Private Events

Wiens Family Cellars can accommodate over 250 guests for private events.

Visit their website or call for more information.

Wilson Creek Winery & Vineyards

35960 Rancho California Rd
Temecula, CA 92591

951-699-9463
www.wilsoncreekwinery.com

Hours

10:00 am-5:00 pm
Open seven days a week

Wine List

Red Wines
Cabernet Sauvignon
Syrah
Zinfandel
Merlot
Petite Syrah
Wilson Family Legacy
Cabernet/Zinfandel
Pinot Mour

White Wines
Golden Jubilee
Chardonnay
Muscat Canelli
Sauvignon Blanc
Riesling
White Cabernet Sauvignon
Viognier
Quartet Blanc

Champagnes
Almond Champagne
Cuvee Champagne

Dessert Wines
Angelica Cream Sherry
Decadencia Chocolate Port

Wine Tasting

$10.00 per person with souvenir wine glass
15% volume discount
Group Wine Tasting (25 person min.)
$13.00 per person plus 20% service charge & sales tax,
includes:
- Sampling of five premium wines and champagne
- Logo wine glass to keep as a souvenir
- Wine crackers for cleansing the palate

Tours

Tours available by appointment

Amenities

Concerts, Comedy dinner Theater, Charity Fundraisers, luaus, grape stomps & cigar nights

Wine Club Information

- 20% discount on bottle purchases
- 25% discount for cases of wine
- 20% merchandise discount
- 40% off cases of Almond Champagne
- 10% Wilson Creek Events discount
- access to pre-releases and special lots.
- Receive personal invitations to join us at elegant dinners, concerts, cruises, outdoor BBQs, tastings and happy hours at the winery.
- Newsletter with your shipment
- Our new members-only Concierge Service

Restaurant

CREEKSIDE GRILLE

Hours: Open Daily 11:00 am - 5:00 pm
Sunday Brunch served 11:00 am - 2:00 pm

Our menus are created with our own hand crafted wines in mind. All are deliciously paired with wine selections, and are the key to our success. We have developed a menu with our guests' sophisticated palette in mind, upscale, yet comfortable items from our appetizers to our desserts.

The Creekside Grille at Wilson Creek Winery features our talented team of chefs to create cuisine utilizing the freshest seasonal local ingredients.

The Creekside Grille's menu offers the best in cuisine to compliment our selection of excellent wines. The menu changes seasonally to savor the bounty of the local farmers and newly released wines. The setting is warm and friendly, with a staff to anticipate your every need.

Weddings & Private Events

Wilson Creek Winery & Vineyards can accommodate up to 300 guests for private events. Visit website for more information.

A Wine Taster's Glossary

Temecula Wineries

A

Acetic
Vinegary taste or smell that develops when a wine is
overexposed to air.

Acidity
All wines naturally contain acids, which should be in
proper balance with fruit and other components. Sufficient
acidity gives liveliness and crispness and is critical for
wines to age.

Aftertaste
The flavor impression the wine leaves after it is swallowed.
Also referred to as the "finish" of a wine. Fine wines have a
lingering finish, or aftertaste.

Aroma
The smell of a wine, especially young wines.

Aromatic
A term for wines with pronounced aroma, particularly
those redolent of herbs or spices.

Astringent
The "puckerish" quality of high tannin content, which has
the effect of drying out the mouth. Many young red wines
are astringent because of tannin.

Austere
Somewhat hard, with restrained fruit and character.

B

Balance
Harmony among the wine's components -- fruit, acidity, tannins, alcohol; a well-balanced wine possesses the various elements in proper proportion to one another.

Big
Powerful in aroma and flavor; full-bodied.

Bitter
Usually considered a fault in but characteristic of such wines as Amarone and certain other Italian reds.

Body
The weight and texture of a wine; it may be light-bodied or full-bodied. Often refers to alcohol content.

Botrytis cinerea
A mold that attacks certain grapes, producing honeyed sweet wines like Sauternes and late-harvest Rieslings.

Bouquet
The complex of aromas that develops with age in fine wines; young wines have aroma, not bouquet.

Breed
Similar to good bloodlines and handling, as in racehorses; the result of soil, grapes and vinification techniques that combine to produce depth and distinctive character in a wine.

Brix
Term used to measure the sugar content of grapes, grape juice (must) or wine. Grapes are generally harvested at 20 to 25 Brix, resulting in alcohol after fermentation of 11.5 to 14 percent.

Brut
Term for dry Champagne or sparkling wine.

Buttery
Descriptor for rich flavor and smoothness of texture, somewhat akin to the oiliness and flavor of butter. More often refers to oak-aged white wines than reds; many Chardonnays and white Burgundies are said to have buttery aromas and flavors.

C

Chewy
Wines with unusual thickness of texture or tannins that one almost "chews" before swallowing.

Clean
Fresh, with no discernible defects; refers to aroma, appearance and flavor.

Closed
Young, undeveloped wines that do not readily reveal their character are said to be closed. Typical of young Bordeaux or Cabernet Sauvignon, as well as other big red wines.

Coarse
Rude or harsh in flavor; clumsy or crude.

Complete
Mature, with good follow-through on the palate, satisfying mouth-feel and firm aftertaste.

Complex
Multifaceted aroma and/or flavor. Most wines considered great exhibit a combination of flavor and aroma elements.

Cooked
Heavy, pruney flavor; also said of wines from very hot growing regions or wines that are overripe.

Corked, corky
Smelling of cork rather than wine; due to a faulty cork.

Crisp
Fresh, brisk character, usually with high acidity.

D

Deep
Having layers of persistent flavor that gradually unfold with aeration.

Delicate
Light fragrance, flavor, and body.

Developed
Mature. A well-developed wine is more drinkable than an undeveloped one.

Distinctive
Elegant, refined character that sets the wine apart on its own.

Dry
Opposite of sweet; somewhat subjective in that tasters may perceive sweetness to varying degree.

Dull
Lacking liveliness and proper acidity; uninteresting.

Dumb
Not revealing flavor or aroma; closed; typical of wines that are too young or too cold.

E

Earthy
Smell or flavor reminiscent of earth. A certain earthiness can be appealing; too much makes the wine coarse.

Elegant
Refined character, distinguished quality, stylish, not heavy.

Extra Dry
A term used on Champagne labels to indicate not-quite-dry; not as dry as Brut.

F

Fat
Full of body and flavor; fleshy.

Fine
Distinguished.

Finesse
Distinctive balance; fineness; elegance and flair.

Finish
Aftertaste, or final impression the wine leaves; it can have a long finish or a short one (not desirable).

Firm
Taut balance of elements; tightly knit structure; also distinct flavor.

Flat
Dull, lacking in liveliness; wine without sufficient acid.

Flavor
How the wine tastes.

Fleshy
Fatness of fruit; big, ripe.

Flinty
Dry, mineral character that comes from certain soils, mostly limestone, in which the wine was grown; typical of French Chablis and Loire Valley Sauvignon Blancs (Sancerre).

Flowery
Aroma suggestive of flowers.

Forward
Developed ahead of its peers; also, when the fruit is prominent, it is said to be forward.

Foxy
The "grapey" flavors of wines made from native American grapes, *Vitis labrusca*.

Fruity
Aroma and/or flavor of grapes; most common to young, light wines but refers also to such fruit flavors in wine as apple, black currant, cherry, citrus, pear, peach, raspberry, or strawberry; descriptive of wines in which the fruit is dominant.

Full-bodied
Full proportion of flavor and alcohol; big, fat.

G

Green
A wine made from unripe grapes that is tart and lacking fruit flavor.

Grip
Firmness of flavor and structure.

H

Hard
Stiff, with pronounced tannins; undeveloped.

Harmonious
All elements -- fruit, acid, tannin -- in perfect balance

Harsh
Rough, biting character from excessive tannin or acid.

Heady
High in alcohol, very full-bodied

Herbaceous
Aromas reminiscent of fresh grass or hay; grassy, as in certain Sauvignon Blancs; also the green pepper character of some Cabernets.

Herby
Reminiscent of herbs, such as mint, sage, thyme, or of eucalyptus.

Honest
Without flaws, typical and straightforward, simple but not great.

Honeyed
Smell or taste reminiscent of honey, characteristic of late-harvest wines affected by "noble rot" (Botrytis cinerea).

I

Intricate
Interweaving of subtle complexities of aroma and flavor.

L

Legs
The viscous rivulets that run down the side of the glass after swirling or sipping, a mingling of glycerin and alcohol.

Length
Lingering aftertaste.

Light
Refers to wines light in alcohol but also to texture and weight, how the wine feels in the mouth. Lightness is appropriate in some wines, a defect in others.

Lively
Crisp, fresh, having vitality.

Long
Fine wines should have a long finish, or aftertaste; see Length.

Luscious
Rich, opulent, and smooth; most often said of sweet wines but also intensely fruity ones.

M

Maderized
Wine that has oxidized; has brown or amber color and stale odor.

Mature
Fully developed, ready to drink.

Meaty
A wine with chewy, fleshy fruit; sturdy and firm in structure.

Mellow
Smooth and soft, with no harshness.

Moldy
Wines with the smell of mold or rot, usually from grapes affected by rot or from old moldy casks used for aging.

Muscular
Vigorous fruit, powerful body and flavor; robust.

Musty
Stale, dusty or rank aromas.

N

Noble
Great; of perfect balance and harmonious expression. The so-called "noble" grapes are those that produce the world's finest wines: Cabernet Sauvignon, Merlot, Chardonnay, Sauvignon Blanc, Semillon and Riesling (some would also include Syrah, Nebbiolo and Sangiovese).

Nose
The smell of the wine; it may have a "good nose" or an "off-nose," meaning defective odors.

Nutty
Nutlike aromas that develop in certain wines, such as sherries or old white wines.

O

Oak, oaky
Aroma and flavor that derive from aging in oak casks or barrels. Characterized by smokiness, vanilla, clove or other spices. Should not be overly pronounced.

Off-dry
Not quite dry, a perception of sweetness too faint to call the wine sweet.

Off-flavors (also off-aromas or off-nose)
Not quite right; flavors or odors that are not correct for a particular type of wine; opposite of clean; defective.

Open
Revealing full character.

Oxidized
Flat, stale or sherry like aroma and flavor; spoiled as the result of overexposure to air.

P

Petillant
A light sparkle.

R

Rich
Full, opulent flavor, body and aroma.

Ripe
Mature, fully ripe fruit.

Robust
Full-bodied, powerful, heady

Rough
Harsh edges, biting, unpleasant.

Round
Smooth and well-developed flavor, without angularity or rough edges.

S

Sharp
Biting acid or tannin.

Short
Refers to finish, or aftertaste, when it ends abruptly.

Silky
Smooth, sinuous texture and finish.

Simple
Opposite of complex; straightforward.

Smoky
Aroma and flavor sometimes associated with oak aging.

Soft
May refer to soft, gentle fruit in delicate wines, or to lack of acidity in wines without proper structure; used on a label occasionally to indicate low alcohol.

Solid
Sound, well structured, firm.

Sour
Sharply acidic or vinegary

Sparkling
Wines with bubbles created by trapped carbon dioxide gas, either natural or injected.

Spicy
Having the character or aroma of spices such as clove, mint, cinnamon, or pepper.

Spritzy
Slight prickle of carbon dioxide, common to some very young wines; frizzante in Italy.

Steely
Firmly structured; taut balance tending toward high acidity.

Stiff
Unyielding, closed; dumb.

Strong
Robust, powerful, big.

Structure
The way a wine is built; its composition and proportions.

Stuffing
Big, flavorful, full-bodied wines are said to have "stuffing."

Sturdy
Bold, vigorous flavor; full-bodied; robust.

Sulphur, SO2
An anti-oxidant used in making most wines; the fermentation process creates minute natural amounts.

Supple
Yielding in flavor; a wine that is readily accessible for current drinking.

Sweet
Usually indicates the presence of residual sugar, retained when grape sugar is not completely converted to alcohol. Even dry wines, however, may have an aroma of sweetness, the combination of intense fruit or ripeness. Considered a flaw if not properly balanced with acidity.

T

Tannin
A natural component found to varying degrees in the skins, seeds and stems of grapes; most prominent in red wines, where it creates a dry, puckering sensation in young reds of concentrated extract; mellows with aging and drops out of the wine to form sediment; a major component in the structure of red wines.

Tart
sharp; acceptable if not too acidic.

Thick
Dense and heavy in texture.

Thin
Lacking body and flavor.

Tired
Past its peak of flavor development; old.

Tough
Astringent or hard; wiry; tannic.

V

Vanilla
A scent imparted by aging in oak.

Velvety
Smooth and rich in texture.

Vigorous
Firm, lively fruit, strong body; assertive flavor.

Vinegary
Having the smell of vinegar; see also Acetic.

Volatile, Volatile Acidity (VA)
Smells of acetic acid and/or ethyl acetate, quite disagreeable when excessive though a tiny amount may enhance aromas.

W

Watery
Thin, lacking in flavor.

Weak
Lacking grip typical for the wine; without character

Weedy
Aromas or flavors reminiscent of hay or grasses; not
necessarily unpleasant unless exaggerated.

Weighty
Strong, powerful, full-bodied, forceful.

Woody
Excessive aromas of wood, common to wines aged
overlong in cask or barrel.

Y

Yeasty
A bready smell, sometimes detected in wines that have
undergone secondary fermentation, such as Champagne;
very appealing if not excessive.

Young
In simple wines signifies youthful freshness; in finer wines,
refers to immaturity, wines as yet undeveloped

Temecula Valley Wine Varietals

Below is a list of the most common Temecula Valley wine varietals and the wineries where they are currently available.

- **Aleatico** – Hart

- **Amante** – Falkner

- **Anglianico** – Cougar

- **Ariana** – Ponte

- **Barbera** – Boorman, Hart, Keyways, Ponte, Temecula Hills

- **Cabernet Franc** – Baily, Boorman, Callaway, Churon, Cougar, Frangipani, Hart, Leonesse, Longshadow, Mount Palomar, Palumbo, Stuart Cellars, Wiens

- **Cabernet Sauvignon** – Alex's Red Barn, Baily, Bella Vista, Boorman, Callaway, Churon, Cougar, Doffo, Falkner, Filsinger, Foote Print, Frangipani, Gershon Bachus, Hart, Keyways, La Cereza, Leonesse, Longshadow, Maurice Car'rie, Miramonte, Mount Palomar, Oak Mountain, Palumbo, Ponte, Rancho de Andallusia, Thornton Robert Renzoni, South Coast, Stuart Cellars, Temecula Hills, Wilson Creek

- **Chardonnay** – Baily, Bella Vista, Callaway, Churon, Cougar, Falkner, Filsinger, La Cereza, Leonesse, Longshadow, Maurice Car'rie, Miramonte, Mount Palomar, Oak Mountain, Ponte, Rancho de Andallusia, Robert Renzoni, South Coast, Stuart Cellars, Temecula Hills, Thornton, Thornton, Wiens, Wilson Creek

- **Charvinier** – Filsinger

- **Chenin Blanc** - Maurice Car'rie

- **Cinsault** - Mount Palomar

- **Claret** – Frangipani

- **Cortese** – Cougar, Mount Palomar

- **Dolcetto** – Callaway, Ponte

- **Frolich** – Keyways

- **Fume Blanc** - Bella Vista, Filsinger, Ponte, Rancho de Andallusia

- **Gamay Noir**

- **Garnacha** - La Cereza

- **Gewurztraminer** – Filsinger, La Cereza, South Coast, Thornton

- **Graciela** – Ponte

- **Grenache** – Frangipani, Miramonte, South Coast, Temecula Hills

- **Magnum** – Doffo, Ponte

- **Malbec** - Churon, Cougar, Doffo, Rancho de Andallusia, Stuart Cellars

- **Meritage** – Baily, Callaway, Cougar, Falkner, Leonesse, Mount Palomar, Oak Mountain, Ponte, South Coast

- **Merlot** – Baily, Bella Vista, Boorman, Callaway, Churon, Cougar, Falkner, Filsinger, Foote Print, Frangipani, Hart, Keyways, La Cereza,

Longshadow, Maurice Car'rie, Miramonte, Mount Palomar, Oak Mountain, Palumbo, Ponte, Rancho de Andallusia, South Coast, Stuart Cellars, Thornton, Wilson Creek

- **Metaphor** – Boorman

- **Mistura** – Doffo

- **Montage** – Baily

- **Moscato** – Ponte, Robert Renzoni, Thornton

- **Mourvedre / Mataro** - Temecula Hills

- **Muscat** - Stuart Cellars

- **Muscat Blanc** – Baily, Longshadow

- **Muscat Canelli** - Alex's Red Barn, Bella Vista, Callaway, Cougar, Leonesse, Maurice Car'rie, South Coast, Temecula Hills, Wilson Creek

- **Opulente** – Miramonte

- **Orange Muscat** – Filsinger

- **Petit Verdot** – Churon, Mount Palomar

- **Petite Syrah** - Bella Vista, Frangipani, Wiens, Wilson Creek

- **Pinot Gris / Grigio** – Callaway, La Cereza, Leonesse, Ponte, Robert Renzoni, Wiens

- **Pinot Mour** - Wilson Creek

- **Pinot Noir** - Stuart Cellars, Wiens

- **Port** – Baily, Callaway, Doffo, Falkner, Foote Print, Keyways, Leonesse, Longshadow, Mount Palomar, Oak Mountain, Ponte, South Coast, Stuart Cellars, Temecula Hills, Wiens

- **Primitivo** – Cougar

- **Riesling** – Alex's Red Barn, Baily, Bella Vista, Cougar, Falkner, Filsinger, Frangipani, Keyways, Leonesse, Maurice Car'rie, Miramonte, Mount Palomar, Ponte, Rancho de Andallusia, South Coast, Stuart Cellars, Thornton, Wilson Creek

- **Roussanne** - South Coast

- **Sangiovese** – Baily, Callaway, Churon, Cougar, Frangipani, La Cereza, Maurice Car'rie, Miramonte, Mount Palomar, Oak Mountain, Palumbo, Rancho de Andallusia, Robert Renzoni, South Coast, Stuart Cellars, Thornton, Wiens

- **Sangria** – Miramonte

- **Sauvignon Blanc** – Alex's Red Barn, Bella Vista, Callaway, Doffo, Falkner, Frangipani, Keyways, Leonesse, Maurice Car'rie, Miramonte, Mount Palomar, Oak Mountain, South Coast, Stuart Cellars, Thornton, Wilson Creek

- **Semillon** – Baily, Miramonte

- **Sherry** - Alex's Red Barn, Maurice Car'rie, Mount Palomar, Wilson Creek

- **Solanus** - Mount Palomar

- **Sonata** - Bella Vista

- **Sparkling Wine/Champagne** – Cougar, Filsinger, La Cereza, Maurice Car'rie, Oak Mountain, South Coast, Temecula Hills, Thornton, Wiens, Wilson Creek

- **Super Tuscan** – Ponte

- **Syrah / Shiraz** - Alex's Red Barn, Callaway, Churon, Doffo, Falkner, Filsinger, Foote Print, Hart, Keyways, La Cereza, Longshadow, Miramonte, Mount Palomar, Palumbo, Rancho de Andallusia, South Coast, Temecula Hills, Thornton, Wiens, Wilson Creek

-

- **Tempranillo** – Filsinger, Hart, Keyways, La Cereza, Ponte, Stuart Cellars, Temecula Hills, Wiens

- **Tre Fratelli** – Palumbo

- **Trovato** - Mount Palomar

- **Ubervin** - Mount Palomar

- **Viognier** - Alex's Red Barn, Bella Vista, Callaway, Churon, Doffo, Falkner, Filsinger, Frangipani, Hart, La Cereza, Miramonte, Mount Palomar, Palumbo, South Coast, Stuart Cellars, Temecula Hills, Thornton, Wiens, Wilson Creek

- **White Cabernet** - Bella Vista, Filsinger, South Coast, Wilson Creek

- **White Merlot** – Leonesse, Longshadow, Oak Mountain, Rancho de Andallusia, South Coast, Stuart Cellars

- **White Zinfandel** - La Cereza, Maurice Car'rie, Thornton

- **Zinfandel** - Bella Vista, Callaway, Filsinger, Foote Print, Frangipani, Gershon Bachus, Hart, Keyways, La Cereza, Leonesse, Miramonte, Oak Mountain, Ponte, Rancho de Andallusia, Robert Renzoni, South Coast, South Coast, Stuart Cellars, Temecula Hills, Thornton, Wilson Creek

* Wine lists are subject to change. Please contact the wineries to confirm their current wine selection.

Map of the Temecula Valley Wine Country

Temecula Wineries

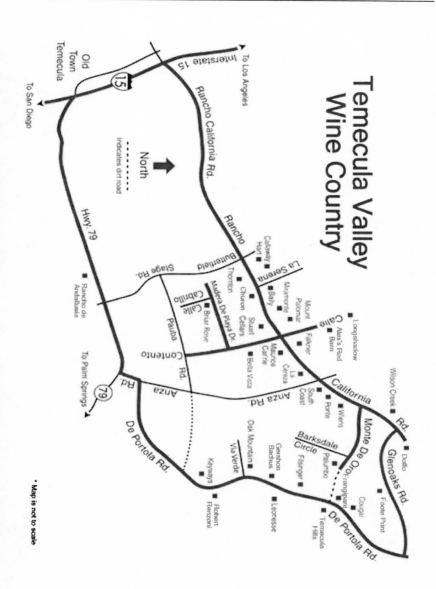

NOTES:

NOTES:

NOTES:

NOTES:

NOTES:

NOTES:

NOTES:

NOTES:

NOTES:

LaVergne, TN USA
30 June 2010
187901LV00002B/20/P